# FOOD LOVERS

# CHINESE

RECIPES SELECTED BY RENE CHAN

Trans
Atlantic
Press

# All recipes serve four people, unless otherwise indicated.

For best results when cooking the recipes in this book, buy fresh ingredients and follow the instructions carefully. Make sure that everything is properly cooked through before serving, particularly any meat and shellfish, and note that as a general rule vulnerable groups such as the very young, elderly people, pregnant women, convalescents and anyone suffering from an illness should avoid dishes that contain raw or lightly cooked eggs.

For all recipes, quantities are given in standard U.S. cups and imperial measures, followed by the metric equivalent. Follow one set or the other, but not a mixture of both because conversions may not be exact. Standard spoon and cup measurements are level and are based on the following:

1 tsp. = 5 ml, 1 tbsp. = 15 ml, 1 cup = 250 ml / 8 fl oz.

Note that Australian standard tablespoons are 20 ml, so Australian readers should use 3 tsp. in place of 1 tbsp. when measuring small quantities.

The electric oven temperatures in this book are given for conventional ovens with top and bottom heat. When using a fan oven, the temperature should be decreased by about 20–40ºF / 10–20ºC – check the oven manufacturer's instruction book for further guidance. The cooking times given should be used as an approximate guideline only.

# CONTENTS

# BEEF WITH BLACK BEANS

## Ingredients

3 tbsp toasted sesame oil, divided

8 shallots, quartered

2 inch / 5-cm piece fresh ginger root, peeled and thinly sliced

2 cloves garlic, thinly sliced

1 head broccoli, stems peeled and cut into small florets

2 heads bok choy, quartered lengthwise

12 oz / 300 g rump steak, thinly sliced and threaded onto skewers

Generous ½ cup / 150 g black bean stir-fry sauce

## Method

Prep and cook time: 20 min

**1** Heat 2 tablespoons of the oil in a large skillet over medium heat. Add the shallots, ginger and garlic and stir-fry for 2 minutes or until just beginning to color.

**2** Add the broccoli and bok choy and stir-fry for 2–3 minutes until wilted, but still crisp. Divide between 4 plates or bowls and keep warm.

**3** Heat the remaining tablespoon oil in the skillet over high heat. Add the steak skewers and cook, turning occasionally, for 2 minutes or until well browned and cooked to your liking. Reduce the heat.

**4** Pour the black bean sauce over the top and add 5 tablespoons of cold water. Cook, stirring gently for 1 minute until the beef is well coated and the sauce is hot. Spoon over the vegetables and serve immediately

# SESAME CHICKEN WITH CASHEWS

## Ingredients

1 egg white

2 tsp cornstarch (cornflour)

½ tsp salt

4 skinless boneless chicken breasts

2 tbsp vegetable oil, divided

1 tbsp black sesame seeds

2 tsp dark soy sauce

2 tsp cider vinegar

2 tsp chili bean sauce

1 tbsp sesame oil

2 tsp sugar

1 tbsp rice wine or dry sherry

4 scallions (spring onions),
roughly chopped

1 red bell pepper, sliced

1 cup / 200 g baby corn,
cut into bite-size pieces

4 tbsp cashew nuts

## Method

Prep and cook time: 35 min

**1** In a medium bowl, whisk together the egg white, cornstarch and salt. Add the chicken and stir to coat. Refrigerate for 15 minutes.

**2** Meanwhile, to prepare the sauce, heat 1 tbsp of the vegetable oil in a small skillet. Add the sesame seeds and stir-fry for 30 seconds until fragrant. Stir in the soy sauce, cider vinegar, chili bean sauce, sesame oil, sugar and rice wine or dry sherry. Bring to a boil, then remove from the heat and set aside.

**3** Bring 1½ cups / 350 ml water to a boil in a large skillet or wok. Add the chicken, reduce the heat and simmer until cooked through. Drain, discarding the water. Add the cooked chicken to the sauce and warm through.

**4** Return the skillet to the heat and add the remaining tablespoon vegetable oil. Add the scallions (spring onion), red bell pepper, corn and cashews and stir-fry until the vegetables are softened, 3–5 minutes.

**5** Divide the vegetable mixture into 4 bowls. Cut each chicken breast into 5 slices and arrange on top of the vegetables. Drizzle with the sesame sauce and serve at once.

# SWEET AND SOUR PORK

## Ingredients

1 tbsp rice wine

1 tbsp light soy sauce

2 tsp sesame oil

1 lb / 450 g pork loin,
cut into cubes

1 egg, lightly beaten

4 tbsp cornstarch (cornflour),
divided

Vegetable oil for deep-frying

For the sauce:

1 large carrot, sliced diagonally

2/3 cup / 150 ml chicken broth
(stock)

1 tbsp light soy sauce

2 tsp dark soy sauce

2 tsp sesame oil

4 tsp rice vinegar

1 tbsp sugar

2 tbsp ketchup

2 tsp cornstarch (cornflour),
mixed to a smooth paste in
1 tbsp water

1 red bell pepper, chopped into
diamonds

4 scallions (spring onions),
trimmed and roughly chopped

To garnish:

Cilantro (fresh coriander) leaves

## Method

Prep and cook time: 40 min

**1** Combine the rice wine, soy sauce and sesame oil in a medium bowl; add the pork and toss to coat. Marinate for 15 minutes.

**2** In a wide shallow bowl, beat the egg with 1 tbsp of the cornstarch (cornflour). Place the remaining 3 tbsp cornstarch in another wide shallow bowl.

**3** Heat the oil in a deep fat fryer to 180°C / 350°F.

**4** Lift the pork from the marinade and toss in the cornstarch to dredge. Then dip the pork into the egg-cornstarch mixture to coat.

**5** Working in batches, deep-fry the pork for about 5 minutes or until golden. Drain on paper towels and keep warm.

**6** For the sauce, cook the carrot in boiling water until softened, 2 minutes; drain and set aside.

**7** In a large skillet or wok, combine the chicken broth (stock), light and dark soy sauce, sesame oil, rice vinegar, sugar, ketchup, and cornstarch and water mixture in a pan and bring to a boil. Cook, stirring, until slightly thickened.

**8** Stir in the carrot, pepper and scallions (spring onions).

**9** Add the fried pork and heat through, stirring gently. Serve at once, garnished with cilantro (coriander) leaves.

# SPICED EGGPLANT

## Ingredients

4 small eggplants (aubergines)

1¹/₃ cups / 300 ml vegetable oil

1 tbsp sugar

2 tbsp rice vinegar

2 tsp soy sauce

2 tbsp rice wine

2 tsp cornstarch (cornflour), mixed to a smooth paste in 1 tbsp water

1 tbsp spicy (hot) bean paste

1 inch / 3-cm piece fresh ginger root, minced

2 cloves garlic, minced

¼ leek, finely chopped

## Method

Prep and cook time: 30 min

**1** Trim the eggplants (aubergines) and cut each lengthwise into 6 wedges.

**2** Heat the oil in a wok or skillet. Add the eggplant in batches and deep-fry for about 3 minutes, until golden brown. Drain on paper towels and keep warm on a plate.

**3** In a small bowl, mix the sugar with the vinegar, soy sauce, rice wine and cornstarch (cornflour) paste to make a sauce.

**4** Pour off and discard the oil in the wok, leaving behind a thin film. Add the bean paste, ginger and garlic and stir-fry for 30 seconds. Stir in the sauce and 1 tbsp water. Bring to a boil and stir in the leeks.

**5** Pour the hot sauce over the eggplant wedges and serve.

# FRIED TOFU WITH MIXED VEGETABLES

## Ingredients

2 tsp vegetable oil, divided

1 lb / 450 g extra firm tofu, cut into cubes

4 shallots, quartered

2 garlic cloves, crushed

1 inch / 3-cm piece fresh ginger root, peeled and grated

1 cup / 200 g baby corn

8 oz / 200 g  snow peas (mangetout)

2 cups / 200 g bean sprouts

8 oz / 200 g oyster and/or shiitake mushrooms, halved if large

1 cup / 225 ml  vegetable broth (stock)

1 tbsp dark brown sugar

1 tbsp light soy sauce

2 tsp cornstarch (cornflour), mixed to a smooth paste in 2 tbsp water

## Method

Prep and cook time: 20 min

**1**  In a nonstick skillet, heat 1 teaspoon of the oil over medium-high heat until hot. Add tofu and cook, gently for about 4 minutes, tossing until lightly golden. Transfer to a plate and set aside.

**2**  Meanwhile, heat the remaining teaspoon of oil in a large skillet or wok. Add the shallots, garlic, ginger, corn, snow peas, bean sprouts and mushrooms. Cook for 5 minutes, stirring frequently.

**3**  Add the tofu to the wok. Pour in the broth (stock), sugar, soy sauce and cornstarch (cornflour) mixture. Heat to boiling and cook for 2 minutes until the sauce thickens. Serve at once.

# SWEETCORN SOUP WITH CRAB MEAT

## Ingredients

1 egg white

1 tsp sesame oil

4 cups / 1 liter chicken broth (stock)

2 cups / 400 g drained canned or thawed frozen corn

1 tbsp rice wine or dry sherry

1 tbsp light soy sauce

2 inch / 5 cm piece fresh ginger root, peeled and grated

1 tsp sugar

Salt and freshly ground pepper, to taste

2 tsp cornstarch (cornflour), mixed to a smooth paste in 1 tbsp water

1½ cups / 250 g flaked crabmeat, picked over to remove shells


To garnish:

2 scallions (spring onions), thinly sliced

1 tbsp chopped cilantro (fresh coriander) leaves

## Method

Prep and cook time: 30 min

**1** In a small bowl, whisk together the egg white and sesame oil; set aside.

**2** Bring the broth (stock) to a boil in a large saucepan. Add the corn and simmer for around 4 minutes.

**3** Add the rice wine or sherry, soy sauce, ginger, sugar, and a little salt and pepper; heat through.

**4** Stir in the cornstarch (cornflour) mixture and bring to a boil, then add the crab.

**5** Slowly add the egg white mixture, stirring constantly; heat through and season with salt and pepper. Serve garnished with scallions (spring onion) and cilantro (coriander).

# CHINESE BROCCOLI WITH ORANGE

## Ingredients

1 head broccoli, stems peeled and cut into small florets

Finely grated zest and juice of 1 orange

2 tsp cornstarch (cornflour)

1 tbsp light soy sauce

½ tsp sugar

2 tbsp olive oil

1 inch / 3-cm piece fresh ginger root, peeled and cut into thin slivers

2 garlic cloves, chopped

1 cup / 100 g bean sprouts

## Method

Prep and cook time: 20 min

**1** Bring a large pot of water to a boil. Add the broccoli and blanch for 30 seconds; drain in a colander under cold running water to stop the cooking. Drain and set aside.

**2** To prepare the sauce, in a small bowl, mix the orange juice and zest with 4 tbsp water, the cornstarch (cornflour), soy sauce and sugar and set aside.

**3** Heat the oil in a wok or large skillet; add the ginger and garlic and stir-fry for 10 seconds. Add the broccoli and stir-fry for 2 minutes more. Add the bean sprouts and cook for 1 more minute.

**4** Stir the orange sauce mixture into the wok and cook, stirring constantly, until the sauce has thickened and coated the broccoli. Spoon into a serving dish and serve at once.

# NOODLES WITH SHRIMP AND VEGETABLES

## Ingredients

1 lb / 450 g Chinese egg noodles

2 tbsp vegetable oil

5 oz / 150 g large shrimp (prawns), peeled, deveined and chopped into bite-size pieces

2 tbsp freshly chopped cilantro (fresh coriander)

1 clove garlic, minced

8 oz / 200 g bok choy, thinly sliced

1 red chili pepper, seeded and sliced into thin strips (wear gloves to prevent irritation)

1 tsp five-spice powder

2 tbsp rice wine or dry sherry

2 tbsp black bean sauce

Soy sauce, to taste

Fish sauce, to taste

## Method

Prep and cook time: 30 min

**1** Cook the noodles according to package instructions. Rinse in a colander under cold running water; drain and set aside.

**2** Heat the oil in a large skillet or wok; add the shrimp and cilantro (coriander) and quickly stir-fry until the shrimp are barely translucent. With a slotted spoon, remove the shrimp from the wok and keep warm.

**3** Return the wok to the heat and add the garlic, bok choy, chili, and five-spice powder; stir to heat through. Add the wine or sherry and about 4 tablespoons of water; bring to a boil, scraping up browned bits from the bottom of the pan.

**4** Add the bean sauce and simmer for around 1–2 minutes, stirring constantly. Stir in the shrimp and noodles and cook, tossing gently to coat, until heated through. Add the soy sauce and fish sauce and season with salt and pepper.

**5** Rest briefly to allow the flavors to mingle, then serve in bowls.

# PORK WITH PLUM SAUCE

## Ingredients

1 lb 12 oz / 800 g pork loin,
cut into strips

2 tsp sesame oil

2 carrots, peeled and sliced into
thin strips

1 clove garlic, minced

1 inch / 3 cm piece fresh ginger root,
peeled and grated

2 tbsp soy sauce, plus more to taste

2–3 tbsp plum sauce


Garnish:

1 scallion (spring onion), thinly sliced
on the diagonal

Chopped fresh parsley

## Method
Prep and cook time: 25 min

**1** Heat the oil in a wok or large skillet until very hot. Add the pork and cook, turning occasionally, until browned on all sides.

**2** Add the carrots, garlic, ginger, soy sauce and a little water; heat through.

**3** Stir in the plum sauce and simmer for 3–4 minutes, stirring occasionally.

**4** Season the meat with soy sauce and serve garnished with scallion (spring onion) and parsley.

# CHICKEN CHOW MEIN

## Ingredients

For the noodles:

8 oz / 225 g dried egg noodles

1 tbsp sesame oil

For the chicken and marinade:

2 tsp light soy sauce

2 tsp rice wine or dry sherry

1 tsp sesame oil

½ tsp salt

½ tsp freshly ground white pepper

4 oz / 100 g skinless boneless chicken breast, cut into matchsticks

For the stir-fry:

3 tbsp vegetable oil, divided

1 tbsp minced garlic

½ cup / 50 g snow peas or sugar snap peas, thinly sliced lengthwise

⅓ cup / 50 g shredded cooked ham

2 tsp light soy sauce

2 tsp dark soy sauce

1 tbsp rice wine or dry sherry

1 tsp salt

½ tsp freshly ground pepper

½ tsp sugar

3 tbsp scallions (spring onions), chopped

1 tsp sesame oil

## Method

Prep and cook time: 40 min

**1** Cook the noodles in a large pot of boiling water for 3–5 minutes, then drain and refresh in cold water. Toss with the sesame oil and set aside.

**2** Combine the soy sauce, rice wine or sherry, sesame oil, salt and white pepper in a medium bowl; add the chicken and toss to coat. Let stand 10 minutes to marinate.

**3** Heat a skillet or wok over high heat. Add 1 tablespoon of the vegetable oil and when very hot and slightly smoking, add the shredded chicken. Stir-fry for about 2 minutes, then transfer to a plate.

**4** Return the wok to the heat, then add the remaining 2 tablespoons vegetable oil. When slightly smoking, add the garlic and stir-fry for 10 seconds. Then add the snow peas or sugar snaps and ham and stir-fry for about 1 minute.

**5** Add the chicken with its juices and the light and dark soy sauce; stir-fry for 3–4 minutes until chicken is nearly cooked. Add the rice wine or sherry, salt, pepper, sugar and scallions. Stir-fry for 2 minutes.

**6** Add the noodles and sesame oil and give the mixture a few final stirs to reheat. Turn onto a warm platter and serve at once.

# SPICY KING PRAWNS

## Ingredients

1 tbsp vegetable oil

1 inch / 3-cm piece fresh ginger, peeled and grated

2 garlic cloves, minced

2 scallions (spring onions) and chopped

1 lb / 450 g raw large shrimp (prawns), peeled and deveined

1 tbsp tomato paste

2 tsp chili bean sauce

1 tsp cider vinegar

1 tsp sugar

2 tsp sesame oil

Cilantro (fresh coriander) leaves, to garnish

## Method
Prep and cook time: 20 min

**1** Heat the oil in a large skillet or wok. Add the ginger, garlic and scallions (spring onions) and stir-fry for 20 seconds.

**2** Add the shrimp (prawns) and stir-fry for 1 minute.

**3** Add the tomato paste, chili bean sauce, cider vinegar, sugar and sesame oil and stir-fry for another few minutes. Serve at once, garnished with cilantro (coriander).

# PORK WITH VEGETABLES AND EGG FRIED RICE

## Ingredients

1 tbsp sesame oil

1 inch / 3 cm piece fresh ginger root, grated

1 clove garlic, minced

1 red onion, sliced

1 lb / 450 g lean pork, cut into strips

1 red bell pepper, coarsely chopped

1 yellow bell pepper, coarsely chopped

4 oz / 100 g chestnut or brown button mushrooms, quartered

2 tbsp sweet chili sauce

2 tbsp dark soy sauce

2 tbsp teriyaki sauce

7 oz / 200 g snow peas (mangetout)

For the fried rice:

1 egg

2 tsp sesame oil

2 tbsp vegetable oil

1 cup / 200 g cooked long-grain rice

½ cup / 400 g thawed frozen peas

4 scallions (spring onions), finely chopped

Salt and freshly ground pepper, to taste

2 tsp light soy sauce

## Method
Prep and cook time: 30 min

**1.** Heat the sesame oil in a large wok or skillet; add the ginger, garlic and onion, stir-fry for 2 minutes.

**2.** Add the pork and fry for 5 minutes, turning as needed, until browned. Add the red and yellow peppers and the mushrooms into the wok and cook, stirring, for another 5 minutes.

**3.** Pour in the sweet chili sauce, soy sauce and teriyaki sauce, then add the snow peas (mangetout). Cook for a further 2–3 minutes; set aside and keep warm.

**4.** For the fried rice, beat together the egg and sesame oil in a small bowl and set aside.

**5.** Heat the vegetable oil in a clean wok or skillet, then add the rice and stir-fry for about 3–4 minutes.

**6.** Add the peas and scallions (spring onions) and stir-fry for about 3 minutes. Season with salt and pepper and splash in the soy sauce, then push to one side of the wok.

**7.** Pour the beaten egg mixture into the other side of the wok and leave for about 10 seconds so it begins to set. Using a chopstick, briskly swirl around the egg to break it up, then toss it gently with the rice. Stir-fry for a further minute and serve at once with the pork and vegetables.

# ROAST PORK WITH VEGETABLES

## Ingredients

For the marinade:

4 tbsp light soy sauce

2 tbsp rice wine or dry sherry

2 tbsp hoisin sauce

2 cloves garlic, minced

1 inch / 3 cm piece fresh ginger root, peeled and grated

3 tbsp honey, divided

1 lb  / 450 g pork loin

For the stir-fry:

2 tbsp sesame oil, divided

4 scallions (spring onions), thinly sliced

4 carrots, sliced into thin sticks

1 red bell pepper, cut into thin strips

7 oz / 200 g snow peas or sugar snap peas, sliced into thin strips

## Method

Prep and cook time: 50 min plus 2 hours marinating

**1**  To prepare the marinade, mix together the soy sauce, rice wine or dry sherry, hoisin sauce, garlic, ginger and 1 tbsp of the honey in a medium bowl. Add the pork to the bowl and turn to coat well. Cover and marinate in the refrigerator for 2 hours.

**2**  Pre-heat the oven to 375°F (190°C / Gas Mark 5). Half fill a roasting pan with water and rest a rack on top.

**3**  In a small bowl, combine the remaining 2 tbsp of honey with 1 tbsp sesame oil and 3 tbsp of the marinade.

**4**  Put the pork onto the rack and brush with the honey-marinade mixture. Roast for 15 minutes, brush over more of the honey marinade and roast for 20 more minutes until the pork is cooked.

**5**  Meanwhile, heat the remaining 1 tbsp sesame oil in a large skillet or wok. Add the scallions, carrots, bell pepper and snow peas or sugar snaps and cook for 5 minutes until the vegetables are slightly softened but still crunchy.

**6**  Bring the remaining marinade to a boil and cook, stirring, until slightly reduced, 5 minutes.

**7**  Slice the pork and serve on a bed of vegetables with a little of the cooked marinade poured over.

# NOODLES WITH VEGETABLES AND GROUND PORK

## Ingredients

4 oz / 100 g thin egg noodles

2 tbsp vegetable oil

12 oz / 350 g ground pork

Soy sauce, to taste

Cayenne pepper, to taste

1–2 tbsp sesame oil

2 cloves garlic, minced

2 scallions (spring onions), thinly sliced

1 inch / 3-cm fresh ginger root, peeled and finely chopped

7 oz / 200 g shiitake mushrooms, quartered

1 cup / 150 g snow peas (mangetout), halved diagonally

1 cup / 150 g thinly sliced Chinese cabbage leaves

2/3 cup / 150 g bamboo shoots, rinsed and drained

## Method

Prep and cook time: 45 min

**1** Cook the noodles in salted water according to package instructions. Rinse in a colander under running water; drain.

**2** Heat the vegetable oil in a large skillet or wok; add the pork and cook, stirring constantly, until no longer pink. Season with soy sauce and cayenne, remove from the skillet and set aside to keep warm.

**3** Return the skillet to the heat and add the sesame oil. Add the garlic, scallions (spring onions), ginger, mushrooms, snow peas (mangetout), cabbage and bamboo shoots and stir-fry for 2–3 minutes.

**4** Add the reserved pork and noodles and continue frying for a further 2 minutes. Season to taste with additional soy sauce and cayenne and serve at once.

# KUNG PAO

## Ingredients

3 tbsp vegetable oil

4 skinless boneless chicken breasts, cut into cubes

3 red chili peppers, seeded and sliced into thin strips

3 garlic cloves, roughly chopped

2 scallions (spring onions), finely chopped

½ cup / 75 g peanuts

1 tsp sugar

2 tbsp rice wine

Soy sauce, to taste

## Method

Prep and cook time: 20 min

**1** In a large skillet or wok, heat the vegetable oil until very hot. Add the chicken and chilies and stir-fry until the chicken is seared, 2–3 minutes.

**2** Add the garlic, scallions (spring onions), peanuts and sugar and continue frying for 1–2 minutes.

**3** Add the rice wine and a little water, if needed, and simmer for 1–2 minutes, until cooked. Season with soy sauce and serve at once.

# CHICKEN WITH OYSTER SAUCE AND NOODLES

## Ingredients

600 g / 1½ lb skinless boneless chicken breasts, chopped into bite-size pieces

Salt and freshly ground pepper, to taste

5 tbsp sesame oil, divided

4-inch / 10-cm piece lemongrass

400 g / 1 lb udon noodles

1 garlic clove, minced

1 scallion (spring onion), finely chopped

3 tbsp oyster sauce

2 tbsp light soy sauce

1 tsp sugar

## Method

Prep and cook time: 20 min plus 30 min to marinate

**1** In a small bowl, mix the chicken with salt, pepper, lemongrass and 2 tbsp of the sesame oil; marinate for 30 minutes.

**2** Cook the noodles in boiling salted water according to package instructions; drain and set aside.

**3** Heat the remaining 3 tbsp oil in a wok or large skillet and stir-fry the garlic and the scallion (spring onion) for 30 seconds. Add the chicken and fry all together for 2–3 minutes, until the chicken is cooked through. Season with oyster sauce, soy sauce and sugar; discard the lemongrass stalk.

**4** Toss the noodles with the chicken and the sauce and heat through; serve at once.

# SICHUAN-STYLE BRAISED FISH

## Ingredients

1 tbsp sunflower or vegetable oil

1 garlic clove, chopped

7 tbsp / 100 ml fish broth (stock)

2 tbsp fish sauce

2 tbsp soy sauce

1 tsp cornstarch (cornflour), mixed to a smooth paste in 1 tbsp water

1 cup / 100 g bean sprouts, fresh or preserved, rinsed and drained

2 lb / 900 g firm white fish fillets, such as cod, plaice or halibut, chopped into 1-inch / 3-cm strips

6 scallions (spring onions), roughly chopped (reserve a few pieces for garnish)

Salt, to taste

Cayenne pepper, to taste

## Method

Prep and cook time: 25 min

**1** Heat the oil in a large skillet or wok; add the garlic and cook, stirring, until softened. Add the fish broth (stock), fish sauce and soy sauce and heat through.

**2** Stir in the cornstarch (cornflour) mixture. Bring to a boil and cook, stirring, until slightly thickened.

**3** Add the bean sprouts, fish and half of the scallions (spring onions), cover and simmer fo 4–5 minutes.

**4** Season with salt and cayenne pepper and serve scattered with the remaining scallions.

# HOT AND SOUR SOUP WITH PORK

## Ingredients

2 tbsp sesame oil

1 lb / 450 g pork loin, sliced into matchsticks

2 chili peppers, seeded and finely chopped (wear gloves to prevent irritation)

1 inch / 3-cm fresh ginger root, peeled and grated

3½ cups / 800 ml strong chicken broth (stock)

3 tbsp rice vinegar

7 oz / 200 g  preserved Mu Err mushrooms, finely sliced*

Soy sauce, to taste

2 tbsp chopped cilantro (fresh coriander) leaves, to garnish

## Method

Prep and cook time: 35 min

**1**  Heat the oil in a skillet or wok. Add the pork and stir-fry until no longer pink, about 1 minute. Transfer to a plate and return the skillet to the heat.

**2**  Add the ginger and chilies and stir-fry 1 minute, then add the broth (stock), vinegar and mushrooms and simmer for around 20 minutes.

**3**  Return the pork and its juices to the soup. Season with soy sauce and serve, sprinkled with cilantro (coriander).


*Preserved Mu Err (wood ear) mushrooms can be found in Asian markets. If unavailable substitute sliced fresh shiitake mushrooms.

# SPICY FISH WITH STIR FRIED VEGETABLES

## Ingredients

1 lb / 450 g firm white fish fillet such as cod or halibut, cut into strips

Salt and freshly ground pepper, to taste

2 tbsp cornstarch (cornflour)

²/₃ cup / 150 ml vegetable oil

1 inch / 3-cm piece fresh ginger root, peeled and grated

2 tbsp sesame oil

3 carrots, thinly sliced on the diagonal

7 oz / 200 g snow peas (mangetout)

4 scallions (spring onions), thinly sliced

2 tbsp rice wine or dry sherry

2 tsp sugar

2 tbsp black bean sauce

2 tbsp sweet chilli sauce

## Method

Prep and cook time: 25 min

**1** Season the fish with salt and ground black pepper and sprinkle over the cornstarch (cornflour) to coat.

**2** Heat the oil in a wok or skillet until very hot then add the fish and fry for a few minutes until almost cooked through.

**3** Remove the fish from the oil with a slotted spoon and drain on paper towels.

**4** Return the wok the heat and fry the ginger for 1 minute then add the sesame oil, heat until smoking and add the carrots.

**5** Stir fry for 2 minutes then add the snow peas (mangetout) and scallions (spring onions) and cook for 1 more minute.

**6** Pour in the rice wine or sherry, sugar, and 2 tbsp of water. Heat through then return the fish to the skillet and cook gently for 1 minute, taking care not to break up the pieces of fish.

**7** Quickly stir through the black bean sauce and chilli sauce and serve immediately.

# FRIED RICE WITH ONIONS, EGG AND MUSHROOMS

## Ingredients

1⅓ cups / 250 g long-grain rice

3 tbsp vegetable oil

8 scallions (spring onions), sliced diagonally into rings (reserve a few for garnish)

2 cups / 250 g halved mushrooms

6 eggs

Freshly ground pepper, to taste

2 tbsp light soy sauce, plus more to taste

Sliced scallion (spring onion), to garnish

## Method

Prep and cook time: 30 min

**1** Cook the rice according to the instructions on the package and let cool completely.

**2** Heat the oil in a wok or skillet. Add the scallion (spring onion) rings and stir-fry for 2 minutes. Add the mushrooms and stir-fry until all liquid has evaporated.

**3** Add the rice and cook, stirring, about 3 minutes, then push the rice mixture to the edges of the wok.

**4** In a small bowl, whisk the eggs and season with pepper and 2 tbsp soy sauce. Pour into the center of the wok and cook quickly, stirring constantly. Lightly mix the eggs through the rice and season with soy sauce, to taste. Scatter with the reserved scallion rings and serve at once.

# ROAST PORK WITH NOODLES

## Ingredients

For the pork and marinade:

1-inch / 3 cm piece fresh ginger root, peeled and grated

4 cloves garlic, crushed

4 tsp superfine (caster sugar)

1 tbsp malt vinegar

½ cup / 100 ml dry sherry

½ cup / 100 ml hoisin sauce

½ cup / 100 ml Chinese barbecue sauce or plum sauce

1 star anise

1 lb / 340 g pork loin


For the noodles:

8 oz / 200 g fine egg noodles

1 tsp sesame oil

1 inch / 3 cm piece fresh ginger root, peeled and grated

2 cloves garlic

1 red chili pepper, seeded and sliced (wear gloves to prevent irritation)

1 tbsp light soy sauce


To garnish:

2 scallions (spring onions), chopped

Bok choy leaves

1 lime, sliced

## Method

Prep and cook time: 50 min plus
12 hours marinating time

**1** Combine the ginger, garlic, sugar, vinegar, sherry, hoisin and barbecue or plum sauces, and star anise in a medium bowl; add the pork and coat well. Cover and marinate in the refrigerator overnight.

**2** Heat the oven to 190C (375F / Gas Mark 5). Half fill a roasting pan with water, and place a roasting rack on top. Take the pork out of the marinade and rest on the rack. Reserve the marinade.

**3** Roast the pork for 15 minutes; turn and baste with a generous amount of the reserved marinade. Roast for 15 minutes more and baste again.

**4** Turn the oven up to 220C (425F / Gas Mark 7) and roast the pork for 10 more minutes. Remove the pork from the oven and allow to rest in a warm place for 10 minutes. Reserve the marinade in the roasting pan and keep warm.

**5** Meanwhile cook the noodles in a pot of boiling salted water for 4 minutes, then drain and rinse in a colander under running water.

**6** Heat the sesame oil in a skillet or wok and fry the ginger, garlic and chili for 30 seconds. Stir in the noodles, add the soy sauce and heat through; set aside.

**7** Thickly slice the pork and serve with the noodles and a little of the reserved marinade spooned over. Garnish with the scallions (spring onions), bok choy leaves and lime slices.

# DUCK BREAST WITH CELERY

## Ingredients

1 tbsp hoisin sauce

2 tbsp rice wine or dry sherry

1 tsp orange juice

½ tsp corn starch (cornflour)

450 g /1 lb skinless boneless duck breasts, sliced into matchsticks

2 tbsp vegetable oil

2 cloves garlic, minced

5 stalks celery, cut into matchsticks

2 scallions (spring onions), thinly sliced

1 red bell pepper, sliced into thin strips

## Method

Prep and cook time: 25 min plus 1 hour to marinate

**1** In a medium bowl, mix the hoisin sauce, rice wine or sherry, the orange juice and cornstarch (cornflour). Add the duck and toss to coat well. Cover and chill for 1 hour.

**2** Heat the oil in a wok or large skillet and stir-fry the garlic for 1 minute.

**3** Add the duck and stir-fry, keeping the heat high, until cooked through, about 5 minutes.

**4** Add the celery, scallions (spring onions) and bell pepper and stir-fry for 2 more minutes, until the vegetables are softened. Serve at once.

Published by Transatlantic Press

First published in 2011

Transatlantic Press
38 Copthorne Road, Croxley Green, Hertfordshire WD3 4AQ

© Transatlantic Press

Images and Recipes by StockFood © The Food Image Agency

Recipes selected by Rene Chan, StockFood

A catalogue record for this book is available from the British Library.

ISBN 978-1-908533-54-8

Printed in China